Second Book of Enoch: 2 Enoch
Also called The Secrets of Enoch
And The Slavonic Book of Enoch

Copyright © 2009 Joseph B. Lumpkin.
All rights reserved.

First time or interested authors, contact Fifth Estate Publishers, Post Office Box 116, Blountsville, AL 35031.

First Printing March, 2009

Cover Design by An Quigley

Printed on acid-free paper

Library of Congress Control No: 2009912933

ISBN: 9781933580814

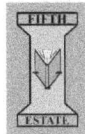

Fifth Estate, 2009

Joseph B. Lumpkin

The Second Book of Enoch: 2 Enoch
Also called The Secrets of Enoch
And The Slavonic Book of Enoch

By Joseph B. Lumpkin

Joseph B. Lumpkin

INTRODUCTION

The study of scripture is a lifelong venture. Many times our search for deeper understanding of the holy book leads to questions beyond the Bible itself. As we encounter references to social conditions, cultural practices, and even other writings mentioned within the scriptures we are called to investigate and expand our knowledge in order to fully appreciate the context, knowledge base, and cultural significance of what is being taught. Thus, to fully understand the Bible, we are necessarily drawn to sources outside the Bible. These sources add to the historical, social, or theological understanding of Biblical times. As our view becomes more macrocosmic, we see the panoramic setting and further understand the full truth within the scriptures.

To point us to the sources we should be concerned with, we must know which books were popular and important at the time of the writing of various books of the Bible. There are several books mentioned in the Bible which are not included in the Bible. They are not spiritual canon, either because they were not available at the time the canon was originally adopted, or at the time they were not considered "inspired." In cases when inspiration was questioned, one could argue that any book quoted or mentioned by a prophet or an apostle should be considered as spiritual canon. Unfortunately this position would prove too simplistic.

Books and writings can fall under various categories such as civil records and laws, historical documents, or spiritual writings. A city or state census is not inspired, but it could add insight into certain areas of life. Spiritual writings which are directly quoted in the Bible serve as insights into the beliefs of the writer or what was considered acceptable by society at the time. As with any new discovery, invention, or belief, the new is interpreted based upon the structure of what came before. This was the way in the first century Christian church as beliefs were based upon the old Jewish understanding. Although, one should realize pagan beliefs were also added to the church as non-Jewish populations were converted, bringing with them the foundations of their beliefs on which they interpreted Christianity. In the case of Jude, James, Paul, and others, the Jewish past was giving way to the Christian present but their understanding and doctrine were still being influenced by what they had learned and experienced previously. It becomes obvious that to understand the Bible one should endeavor to investigate the books and doctrines that most influenced the writers of the Bible.

The Dead Sea Scrolls found in the caves of Qumran are of great interest in the venture of clarifying the history and doctrine in existence between biblical times and the fixing of canon. Many of the scrolls were penned in the second century B.C. and were in use at least until the destruction of the second temple in 70 A.D. Similar scrolls to those found in the eleven caves of Qumran were also found at the Masada stronghold which fell in 73 A.D. Fragments of every book of the Old Testament except Esther were found in the caves of Qumran, but so were many other books. Some of these books are considered to have been of equal importance and influence to the people of Qumran and to the writers and scholars of the time. Some of those studying the scrolls found in Qumran were the writers of the New Testament.

Knowing this, one might ask which of the dozens of non-canonical books most influenced the writers of the New Testament. It is possible to ascertain the existence of certain influences within the Bible context by using the Bible itself. The Bible can direct us to other works in three ways. The work can be mentioned by name, as is the Book of Jasher. The work can be quoted within the Bible text, as is the case with the Book of Enoch. The existence of the work can be alluded to, as is the case of the missing letter from the apostle Paul to the Corinthians.

In the case of those books named in the Bible, one can set a list as the titles are named. The list is lengthier than one might first suspect. Most of these works have not been found. Some have been unearthed but their authenticity is questioned. Others have been found and the link between scripture and scroll is generally accepted. Following is a list of books mentioned in the Holy Bible.

The Book of Jasher: There are two references to the book in the Old Testament:

2 Samuel 1:18 – Also he bade them teach the children of Judah the use of the bow: behold, it is written in the book of Jasher.

Joshua 10:13 - Is it not written in the Book of Jasher? And the sun stopped in the middle of the sky and did not hasten to go down for about a whole day.

There are several books which have come to us entitled, "Book of Jasher." One is an ethical treatise from the Middle Ages. It begins with a section on the Mystery of the Creation of the World: It is clearly unrelated to the Biblical Book of Jasher.

Another was published in 1829 supposedly translated by Flaccus Albinus Alcuinus. It opens with the Chapter 1 Verse 1 reading: "While it was the beginning, darkness overspread the face of nature." It is now considered a fake.

The third and most important is by Midrash, first translated into English in 1840. It opens with Chapter 1 Verse 1 reading: "And God said, Let us make man in our image, after our likeness, and God created man in his own image." A comparison of Joshua 10:13 with Jasher 88:63-64 and 2Sam. 1:18 with Jasher 56:9 makes it clear that this Book of Jasher at least follows close enough with the Bible to be the Book of Jasher mentioned in the Bible. A translation of The Book of Jasher is available from Joseph Lumpkin, published by Fifth Estate.

Other books mentioned by name in the Bible are:

1.   The Book of Wars of the Lord: "Therefore it is said in the Book of the Wars of the Lord." Num. 21:14

2.   The Annals of Jehu: "Now the rest of the acts of Jehoshaphat, first to last, behold, they are written in the annals of Jehu the son of Hanani, which is recorded in the Book of the Kings of Israel." 2 Chronicles 20:34

3.   The treatise of the Book of the Kings: "As to his sons and the many oracles against him and the rebuilding of the house of God, behold, they are written in the treatise of the Book of the Kings. Then Amaziah his son became king in his place." 2 Chronicles 24:27

4.   The Book of Records, Book of the Chronicles of Ahasuerus: "Now when the plot was investigated and found to be so, they were both hanged on a gallows; and it was written in the Book of the Chronicles in the king's presence." ... "During that night the king could not sleep so he gave an order to bring the book of records, the chronicles, and they were read before the king." Esther 2:23; 6:1

5.   The Acts of Solomon: "Now the rest of the acts of Solomon and whatever he did, and his wisdom, are they not written in the book of the Acts of Solomon?" 1 Kings 11:41

6.   The Sayings of Hozai: "His prayer also and how God was entreated by him, and all his sin, his unfaithfulness, and the sites on which he built high places and erected the Asherim and the carved images, before he humbled himself, behold, they are written in the records of the Hozai." 2 Chronicles 33:19

7.   The Chronicles of David: "Joab the son of Zeruiah had begun to count them, but did not finish; and because of this, wrath came upon Israel, and the number was not included in the account of the Chronicles of King David." 1 Chronicles 27:24

8.   The Chronicles of Samuel, Nathan, Gad: "Now the acts of King David, from first to last, are written in the Chronicles of Samuel the seer, in the Chronicles of Nathan the prophet and in the Chronicles of Gad the seer." 1 Chronicles 29:29

9.   Samuel's book: "Then Samuel told the people the ordinances of the kingdom, and wrote them in the book and placed it before the Lord." 1 Samuel 10:25

10.   The Records of Nathan the prophet: "Now the rest of the acts of Solomon, from first to last, are they not written in the Records of

Nathan the prophet, and in the prophecy of Ahijah the Shilonite, and in the visions of Iddo the seer concerning Jeroboam the son of Nebat?" 2 Chronicles 9:29

11.   The Prophecy of Ahijah the Shilonite: "Now the rest of the acts of Solomon, from first to last, are they not written in the Records of Nathan the prophet, and in the prophecy of Ahijah the Shilonite, and in the visions of Iddo the seer concerning Jeroboam the son of Nebat?" 2 Chronicles 9:29

12.   The Treatise of the Prophet Iddo: "Now the rest of the acts of Abijah, and his ways and his words are written in the treatise of the prophet Iddo." 2 Chronicles 13:22

The existence of a book can be inferred as well, this is clearly seen with several missing epistles.

Paul's letter to the church at Laodicea: "When this letter is read among you, have it also read in the church of the Laodiceans; and you, for your part read my letter that is coming from Laodicea." Colossians 4:16 (Since three earlier manuscripts do not contain the words "at Ephesus" in Eph 1:1, some have speculated that the letter coming from Laodicea was in fact the letter of Ephesians. Apostolic fathers also debated this possibility.)

In Paul's first letter to Corinth, he predated that letter by saying: "I wrote you in my letter not to associate with immoral people" (1 Corinthians 5:9) (This could merely be a reference to the present letter of 1 Corinthians.)

Of all the books quoted, paraphrased, or referred to in the Bible, the Book of Enoch has influenced the writers of the Bible as few others have. Even more extensively than in the Old Testament, the writers of the New Testament were frequently influenced by other writings, including the First Book of Enoch.

Since it appears that the author of the Second Book of Enoch had read and was drawing on the First Book of Enoch, or 1 Enoch, we will briefly touch on First Enoch before introducing Second Enoch.

To make things more interesting, there are actually three major works attributed to Enoch. We call these books, 1 Enoch, 2 Enoch, and 3 Enoch. Translations of the other Books of Enoch, including 1 Enoch, 2 Enoch, 3 Enoch, and a single volume containing all three books are available from Joseph Lumpkin and are published by Fifth Estate.

It is not the purpose of this work to make judgments as to the validity or worth of the Books of Enoch, but rather to simply put forth a meaningful question. Is not the non-canonical book that most influenced the thought and theology of the writers of the New Testament worth further research and contemplation?

Most scholars date the First Book of Enoch to sometime during the second century B.C. We do not know what earlier oral tradition, if any, the book contains. 1 Enoch was considered inspired and authentic by certain Jewish sects of the first century B.C. and remained popular for at least five hundred years. The earliest Ethiopian text was apparently derived from a Greek manuscript of the Book of Enoch, which itself was a copy of an earlier text. The original was apparently written in the Semitic language, now thought to be Aramaic.

The First Book of Enoch was discovered in the 18th century. It was assumed to have been penned after beginning of the Christian era. This theory was based upon the fact that it had quotes and paraphrases as well as concepts found in the New Testament. Thus, it was assumed that it was heavily influenced by writers such as Jude and Peter.

However, recent discoveries of copies of the book among the Dead Sea Scrolls found at Qumran prove the book was in existence long before the time of Jesus Christ. These scrolls force a closer look and reconsideration. It becomes obvious that the New Testament did not influence the Book of Enoch; on the contrary, the Book of Enoch influenced the New Testament. The date of the original writing upon which the second century B.C. Qumran copies were based is shrouded in obscurity. Likewise lost are the sources of the oral traditions that came to be the Book of Enoch.

It has been largely the opinion of historians that the book does not really contain the authentic words of the ancient Enoch, since he would have lived several thousand years earlier than the first known appearance of the book attributed to him. However, the first century Christians accepted the Book of 1 Enoch as inspired, if not authentic. They relied on it to understand the origin and purpose of many things, from angels to wind, sun, and stars. In fact, many of the key concepts used by Jesus Christ himself seem directly connected to terms and ideas in the Book of 1 Enoch.

It is hard to avoid the evidence that Jesus not only studied the book, but also respected it highly enough to allude to its doctrine and content. Enoch is replete with mentions of the coming kingdom and other holy themes. It was not only Jesus who quoted phrases or ideas from Enoch, there are over one hundred comments in the New Testament which find precedence in the First Book of Enoch or 1 Enoch.

Other evidence of the early Christians' acceptance of the Book of Enoch was for many years buried under the King James Bible's mistranslation of Luke 9:35, describing the transfiguration of Christ: "And there came a voice out of the cloud, saying, 'This is my beloved

Son. Hear him.' " Apparently the translator here wished to make this verse agree with a similar verse in Matthew and Mark. But Luke's verse in the original Greek reads: "This is my Son, the Elect One (from the Greek ho eklelegmenos, lit., "the elect one"). Hear him."

The "Elect One" is a most significant term (found fourteen times) in the Book of 1 Enoch. If the book was indeed known to the apostles of Christ, with its abundant descriptions of the Elect One who should "sit upon the throne of glory" and the Elect One who should "dwell in the midst of them;" then the great scriptural authenticity is justly accorded to the Book of Enoch when the "voice out of the cloud" tells the apostles, "This is my Son, the Elect One,"... the one promised in the First Book of Enoch.

The Book of Jude tells us in Verse 14 that "Enoch, the seventh from Adam, prophesied." Jude also, in Verse 15, makes a direct reference to the Book of Enoch (2:1), where he writes, "to execute judgment on all, to convict all who are ungodly." As a matter of fact, it is a direct, word for word quote. Therefore, Jude's reference to the Enochian prophesies strongly leans toward the conclusion that these written prophesies were available to him at that time.

Fragments of ten Enoch manuscripts were found among the Dead Sea Scrolls. The number of scrolls indicate the Essenes (a Jewish commune or sect at the time of Christ) could well have used the Enochian writings as a community prayer book or teacher's manual and study text.

Many of the early church fathers also supported the Enochian writings. Justin Martyr ascribed all evil to demons whom he alleged to be the offspring of the angels who fell through lust for women; directly referencing the Enochian writings.

Athenagoras (170 A.D.), regarded 1 Enoch as a true prophet. He describes the angels who "violated both their own nature and their office." In his writings, he goes into detail about the nature of fallen angels and the cause of their fall, which comes directly from the Enochian writings.

In 1773, rumors of a surviving copy of the book drew Scottish explorer James Bruce to distant Ethiopia. He found the Book of Enoch had been preserved by the Ethiopian church, which put it right alongside the other books of the Bible.

Bruce secured not one, but three Ethiopian copies of the book and brought them back to Europe and Britain. In 1773 Bruce returned from six years in Abyssinia. In 1821 Richard Laurence published the first English translation. For more information on 1 Enoch, see "The Lost Book of Enoch.

Later, another Book of Enoch surfaced. This text, dubbed "2 Enoch" or "Second Enoch," and commonly called "the Slavonic Enoch," was discovered in 1886 by Professor Sokolov in the archives of the

Belgrade Public Library. It appears that just as "Ethiopian Enoch" ("1 Enoch") escaped the sixth-century Church suppression of certain texts in the Mediterranean area, so also did "Slavonic Enoch" survive by being propagated in another language long after the original form, from which it was copied, was destroyed or hidden.

The Books of Enoch seems to be a missing link between Jewish and Christian theology. 2 Enoch is considered by many to be more Christian in its theology than Jewish, due to additions made by Christians after the time of its original authorship.

Specialists in the Enochian texts believe that the missing original from which the Slavonic was copied was probably a Greek manuscript, which itself may have been based on a Hebrew or Aramaic manuscript.

The Slavonic text has evidence of many later additions to the original manuscript. Unfortunately, later additions and deletions of teachings considered "erroneous," rendered the text unreliable.

Because of references to dates and data regarding certain calendar systems in the Slavonic Enoch, some claim the text cannot be earlier than the seventh century A.D. Some see these passages not as evidence of Christian authorship, but as later Christian interpolations into an earlier manuscript. This idea seems logical since other data indicates the foundation work for the book may have been written soon after 1 Enoch, but has been since modified greatly. Enochian specialist R.H. Charles, for instance, believes that even the better of the two Slavonic manuscripts contains interpolations and is, in textual terms, "corrupt." However, the book still contains a large amount of information, including the theology and beliefs of certain groups in the time of its authorship, or at least throughout the time of its evolution toward the version we have today.

Introduction to The Second Book of Enoch: Slavonic Enoch

As part of the Enochian literature, The Second Book of Enoch is included in the pseudepigraphal corpus.

Pseudepigrapha | ˌsoōdə¹pigrəfə | Spurious or pseudonymous writings, especially Jewish writings ascribed to various biblical patriarchs and prophets but composed within approximately 200 years of the birth of Jesus Christ.

As stated before, the text known as "Second Enoch," was discovered in 1886 by Professor Sokolov in the archives of the Belgrade Public Library. The book was unknown to the general public and completely unheard of in any other location. The Second Book of Enoch, or 2 Enoch was likely written in the latter half of the first century A.D. but had gone through alterations and additions to make it more acceptable to the Christian community. The text was written in Slavonic but had evidence of being translated from another language. The text has also been known by the titles of "2 Enoch", and "The Secrets of Enoch." 2 Enoch is basically an expansion of Genesis 5:21-32, taking the reader from the time of Enoch to the onset of the great flood of Noah's day.

19

The main theme of the book is the ascension of Enoch progressively through multiple heavens. During the ascension Enoch is transfigured into an angel and granted access to the secrets of creation. Enoch is then given a 30 day grace period to return to earth and instruct his sons and all the members of his household regarding everything God had revealed to him. The text reports that after period of grace an angel will then come to retrieve him to take him from the earth. In the book of 3 Enoch we will be told more about Metatron, the angel that Enoch became.

Many credible versions end with chapter 68, however there is a longer version of 2 Enoch, which we will examine. In this version the wisdom and insights given to the family of Enoch is passed from family members to Melchizedek, whom God raises up as an archpriest. Melchizedek then fulfills the function of a prophet-priest. To pave the way to Melchizedek, Methuselah functions as a priest for ten years and then passed his station on to Nir, Noah's younger brother. Nir's wife, Sopanim, miraculously conceives without human intercourse while about to die and posthumously gives birth to Melchizedek, who is born with the appearance and maturity of a three-year old child and the symbol of the priesthood on his chest.

The world is doomed to suffer the flood but Michael the archangel promises Melchizedek salvation. This establishes his priesthood for all of eternity. The text goes on to report that in the last generation, there will be another Melchizedek who will be "the head of all, a great archpriest, the Word and Power of God, who will perform miracles, greater and more glorious than all the previous ones".

The manuscripts, which contain and preserve this document, exist only in the Old Slavonic language. After the first manuscript was found a search was conducted for any other copies. Of the twenty or more manuscripts dating from the 13th century A.D. no single one contains the complete text of 2 Enoch. When pieced together there appears to be two versions. These we will refer to as the long and short version.

The difference in length between the two is due to two quite different features. There are blocks of text found only in the longer manuscripts; but even when the passages are parallel, the longer manuscripts tend to be more full and detailed. At the same time there is so much verbal similarity when the passages correspond that a common source must be supposed.

The form of 2 Enoch is what one finds in Jewish Wisdom literature and Jewish Apocalyptic literature. It has been suggested that the longer version is characterized by editorial expansions and Christian interpolations. Hence, the shorter version contains fewer Christian elements. The author of 2 Enoch speaks much of the Creator and final judgment, but he speaks very little about redemption, which seems to be absent from the thoughts of the author. Indeed, there seems to be a total lack of a Savior or Redeemer in 2 Enoch. What is noteworthy is that 2 Enoch has no reference to the mercy of God.

In the long version presented here, it appears that the last portion of the text was added as an afterthought. It contains the rise of Melchizedek. The appearance of Melchizedek ties 2 Enoch to several other texts forming a Melchizedkian tradition. The author of 2 Enoch follows a tradition in which an aged mother, who had been barren up to her deathbed, miraculously conceived Melchizedek without human intervention. Before she was able to give birth to the baby she died. The baby then emerged from her dead body with the maturity of a three-year-old boy. His priesthood will be perpetuated throughout the generations until "another Melchizedek" appears. If the last Melchizedek serves as the archpriest for the last generation, it indicates that in the mind of this Jewish writer, the Temple was to be rebuilt and would be the place were God would meet His people when the heathen nations were destroyed. The continuation and victory of the Jews as the selected and blessed people of God is implied. In this vein, 2 Enoch follows certain apocalyptic writings.

(For more information on apocalyptic writings see "End of Days" by Joseph Lumpkin.)

The Slavonic version is translated from a Greek source. Most scholars agree that there was either a Hebrew or Aramaic original lying behind the Greek source from which the Slavonic manuscripts were produced. The Hebrew origins are indicated by "Semitisms" in the work, but there are also Greek words and expressions, such as the names of the planets in chapter 30.

Proof that The Slavonic Enoch was first written in Greek is shown by the derivation of Adam's name, and by several coincidences with the Septuagint. The origin of the story is perhaps based on Hebrew traditions and certain Semitic turns of language show up in the text. This tends to indicate that there was at one time a Hebrew or Aramaic text that preceded the Greek. From the Greek it was translated into Slavonic. Of this version there are five manuscripts, or pieces thereof, found.

The short version or the Slavonic Enoch was probably written by a single author in an attempt to bring all the current traditions about Enoch of his time into a central storyline and system. The schema to accomplish the unity of traditions implements Enoch's ascension through multiple heavens. The heavenly journey is also seen in 1 Enoch and 3 Enoch. This author was probably a Jew living in Egypt. There are several elements in the book, which indicate Egyptian origin. The longer version of 2 Enoch was seeded with Christian elements and appended with an ending that does not fit well, illuminating the fact that there were several authors involved in the longer version.

Parts of the book were probably written in the late first century A.D. The first date is a limit set by the fact that Ethiopic Enoch,

Ecclesiasticus, and Wisdom of Solomon are used as sources or references within the text; the second date is a limit set by the fact that the destruction of the Temple is not mentioned at all. However, it must be added that apocalyptic literature bloomed in the time after the destruction of the temple in the late first century and throughout the second century A.D.

The Slavonic Enoch furnishes new material for the study of religious thought in the beginning of the Common Era. The ideas of the millennium and of the multiple heavens are the most important in this connection. Another very interesting feature is the presence of evil in heaven, the fallen angels in the second heaven, and hell in the third. The idea of evil in heaven may be a nod to the book of Job and the dialog between God and Satan, who was coming and going between heaven and earth. The idea of hell in the third heaven may have been derived from ideas expressed in the Old Testament book of Isaiah, which mentions that the sufferings of the wicked will be witnessed by the righteous in paradise.

Chapter 21 and forward for several chapters shows a heavy influence of Greek mythology. The Zodiac is mentioned along with celestial bodies with names such as Zeus, Cronus, Aphrodite, and others. The part of the text containing names and astrological descriptions could have been tampered with as late as the seventh century A.D.

By far, the most interesting and confusing section begins around chapter 25 and runs for several chapters. Here the text takes a turn toward Gnostic theology and cosmology. The Gnostics were a Christian sect, which formed and grew in the first century A.D. and thrived in the second century A.D.

Although Gnostic borrowed from Plato's (428 B.C. – 348 B.C.) creation myth, the maturity and construction of the story shows it to be of Gnostic Christian origin, placing it no earlier than the last part of the first century A.D. and no later than the end of the Second century. Add to the dating question the fact that the destruction of the Temple in Jerusalem is not mentioned, which leads to a date just before 70 A.D., if one assumes the Gnostic flavor was not added later.

The history of the text is obviously long and varied. It probably began as a Jewish oral tradition with pieces taken from several Enochian stories. Although it was first penned in Hebrew or Aramaic in the first or second century A.D. The date of this incarnation of the text is unknown. Later, the story was further expanded and embellished by Greek influences. Lastly, Christians and Gnostics commandeered the book and added their own matter. Thus 2 Enoch exhibits a kaleidoscope of cultural and religious contributions over a great scope of time from the first century B.C. (assuming it came after 1 Enoch) and ending as late as the seventh century A.D. These additions would allow any serious student insight into how ancient texts evolve.

Second Enoch was rediscovered and published in the early 19th century A.D The text before you uses the R. H. Charles and W. R. Morfill translation of 1896 with additions from other sources. Archaic terms and sentence structure were revised or explained to convey a more modern rendering for the twenty-first century readers.

2 Enoch

Slavonic Enoch

The Book of the Secrets of Enoch

Chapter 1

1 There was a wise man and a great craftsman, and the Lord formed a love for him and received him, so that he should see the highest dwellings and be an eye-witness of the wise and great and inconceivable and unchanging realm of God Almighty, and of the very wonderful and glorious and bright and manifold vision of the position of the Lord's servants, and of the inaccessible throne of the Lord, and of the degrees and manifestations of the spiritual (non-physical) hosts, and of the unspeakable ministration of the multitude of the elements, and of the various apparition and singing of the host of Cherubim which is beyond description, and of the limitless light.

2 At that time, he said, when my one hundred and sixty-fifth year was completed, I begat my son Methuselah.

3 After this I lived two hundred years and finished of all the years of my life three hundred and sixty-five years.

4 On the first day of the month I was in my house alone and was resting on my bed and slept.

5 And when I was asleep, great distress came up into my heart, and I was weeping with my eyes in sleep, and I could not understand what this distress was, or what was happening to me.

6 And there appeared to me two very large men, so big that I never saw such on earth. Their faces were shining like the sun, their eyes were like a burning light, and from their lips fire was coming out. They were singing. Their clothing was of various kinds in appearance and was purple. Their wings were brighter than gold, and their hands whiter than snow.

7 They were standing at the head of my bed and began to call me by my name.

8 And I arose from my sleep and clearly saw the two men standing in front of me.

9 And I greeted them and was seized with fear and the appearance of my face was changed to terror, and those men said to me:

10 Enoch, have courage and do not fear. The eternal God sent us to you, and you shall ascend today with us into heaven, and you shall tell your sons and all your household all that they shall do without you on earth in your house, and let no one seek you until the Lord returns you to them.

11 And I hurried to obey them and went out of my house, and went to the doors, as I was ordered, and I summoned my sons Methuselah and Regim and Gaidad and explained to them all the marvels the men had told me.

Chapter 2

1 Listen to me, my children, I do not know where I will go, or what will befall me. So now, my children, I tell you, do not turn from God in the face of that which is empty or prideful, which did not make heaven and earth, for these shall perish along with those who worship them, and may the Lord make your hearts confident in the fear (respect) of him. And now, my children, let no one consider seeking me, until the Lord returns me to you.

Chapter 3

1 (It came to pass, when Enoch had finished speaking to his sons, that the angels took him on to their wings and lifted him up on to the first heaven and placed him on the clouds.)
And there I (Enoch) looked, and again I looked higher, and saw the ether, and they placed me on the first heaven and showed me a very large sea, bigger than the earthly sea. (See Cor. 12:2. See 1 Enoch.)

Chapter 4

1 They brought the elders and rulers of the stellar orders in front of me, and showed me two hundred angels, who rule the stars and services of the stars to the heavens, and fly with their wings and come round all those who sail.

Chapter 5

1 And here I looked down and saw the storehouses of snow, and the angels who keep their amazing storehouses, and the clouds where they come out of and into which they go. (See 1 Enoch 69:24)

Chapter 6

1 They showed me the storehouse of the dew, like olive oil in its appearance and its form, as of all the flowers of the earth. And they also showed me many angels guarding the storehouses of these things, and how they are made to shut and open. (See 1 Enoch 69:23)

Chapter 7

1 And those men took me and led me up on to the second heaven, and showed me darkness, greater than earthly darkness, and there I saw prisoners hanging, watched, (guarded,) awaiting the great and limitless judgment, and the spirits were dark in appearance, more than earthly darkness, and perpetually weeping through all hours.
2 And I said to the men who were with me: Why are these being unceasingly tortured? They answered me: These are God's apostates, who did not obey God's commands, but took counsel with their own will, and turned away with their prince, who is also held captive in the fifth heaven.
3 And I felt great pity for them, and they greeted me, and said to me: Man of God, pray to the Lord for us. And I answered them: I am just a mortal man. Who am I that I should pray for spirits? Who knows where I go or what will become of me? Or who will pray for me?

Chapter 8

1 And those men took me from there and led me up on to the third heaven, and placed me there. I looked down and saw what this place produces and that it was so good that such as has never been known.

2 And I saw all the sweet, flowering trees and I saw their fruits, which were sweet smelling, and I saw all the foods that came from them and that the food was bubbling with fragrant vapors.

3 And in the middle of the trees was the tree of life, in that place where the Lord rests when he goes up into paradise. And this tree is of indescribable goodness and fragrance, and adorned more than anything existing. And all sides of its form were golden and brilliant red and fire-like and it was completely covered, and it produced all fruits. (See Rev. 22:2)

4 Its root is in the garden at the earth's end.

5 And paradise resides between spiritual and physical.

6 And two springs come out which send forth honey and milk, and their springs send forth oil and wine, and they separate into four parts, and flow quietly around, and go down into the paradise of Eden, between the mutable and the eternal. (See Gen. 2:11-14)

7 And there they go forth along the earth, and have a circular flow even as other elements.

8 And there is no unfruitful tree here, and every place is blessed.

9 Three hundred angels, which are very bright, are there to keep the garden, and with incessant sweet singing with voices, which are never silent, serve the Lord throughout all the hours of days.

10 And I said: How very sweet is this place, and those men said to me:

Chapter 9

1 This place, O Enoch, is prepared for the righteous, who endure all manner of offence from those that exasperate their souls, who avert their eyes from iniquity, and make righteous judgment, and give bread to the hungering, and cover the naked with clothing, and raise up the fallen, and help injured orphans, and who walk without fault before the face of the Lord, and serve him alone, and for them is prepared this place for eternal inheritance.

Chapter 10

1 And those two men led me up on to the Northern side, and showed me there a very terrible place, and there were every kind of tortures in that place: cruel darkness and gloom, and there was absolutely no light at all there, but murky fire constantly flaming above, and there is a fiery river coming out, and everywhere in that entire place is fire, and everywhere there is frost and ice, thirst and shivering, while the physical restraints are very cruel, and the spirits were fearsome and merciless, bearing angry weapons, torturing without mercy.
2 And I said: Woe, woe! This place is so terrible.
3 And those men said to me: This place, O Enoch, is prepared for those who dishonor God, who on earth practice sin against nature, which is sodomy of a child, corruption of children, performing magic, enchantments and devilish witchcrafts, and who boast of their

wicked deeds, stealing, lying, slander, envy, resentment, fornication, murder, and who are accursed and steal the souls of men, and those who see the poor and still take away their goods so they grow rich, and injure them for other men's goods. And this is reserved for those who, to satisfy their own emptiness made the hungering die; those who clothe themselves by stripping the naked; and who did not know their creator, but instead bowed to lifeless gods who have no soul who cannot see nor hear, who are empty, and who built carved images and bow down to unclean fashioning of useless gods, this place is prepared for these as an eternal inheritance.

Chapter 11

1 Those men took me, and led me up on to the fourth heaven, and showed me the entire succession of activities, and all the rays of the light of sun and moon. (See 1 Enoch 72:1-37 and 73:1-8)

2 And I measured their progression, and compared their light, and saw that the sun's light is greater than the moon's.

3 Its circle and the wheels on which it goes always is like the wind passing with very amazing speed with no rest day or night.

4 Its egress and ingress are accompanied by four huge stars, and each star has a thousand stars under it, to the right of the sun's wheel there are four thousand stars and to the left are four thousand, altogether eight thousand, going out with the sun continually.

5 And by day fifteen groups of ten thousand angels attend it, and by night there were a thousand.

6 And six-winged ones go fourth with the angels before the sun's wheel into the fiery flames, and a hundred angels kindle the sun and set it alight.

Chapter 12

1 And I looked and saw other flying elements of the sun, whose names are Phoenixes and Chalkydri, which are marvelous and wonderful, with feet and tails of a lion, and a crocodile's head, they appear to be purple in color like that in the rainbow; their size is nine hundred measures, their wings are like those of angels, each has twelve wings, and they attend and accompany the sun, bearing heat and dew, as it is ordered them from God.

(Note: The word CHALKYDRI means "serpents". It appears that the Slavonic translators rendered the Hebrew word SERAPHIM differently in various places in the text. The word was translated "Serpent" in some places and SERAPHIM in others. The word "Seraph" means "to burn.")

2 This is how the sun revolves and goes, and rises under the heaven, and its course goes under the earth with the light of its rays continually.

Chapter 13

1 Then those men carried me away to the east, and placed me at the sun's gates, where the sun has egress according to the seasons circuit

and regulation of the months of the whole year, and the number of the hours day and night.

2 And I saw six gates open, each gate having sixty-one stadia (185 meters) and A quarter of one stadium (46.25 meters), and I measured them accurately, and knew their size. Through the gates the sun goes out, and goes to the west, and is made even, and rises throughout all the months, and turns back again from the six gates according to the succession of the seasons. In this way the period of the entire year is finished after the return of the four seasons.

(Note: 6 X 61=366 With the quarter day added, this is the length of the leap year.)

Chapter 14

1 And again those men led me away to the western parts, and showed me six great open gates corresponding to the eastern gates, opposite to where the sun sets, according to the number of the days three hundred and sixty-five and a quarter.

(Note that this is a solar calendar of the same length as our modern calendar.)

2 Again it goes down to the western gates, and diminishes (pulls away) its light with the prominent brightness, under the earth. The crown of its glory is in heaven with the Lord, and it is guarded by four hundred angels while the sun goes round on wheel under the

earth. And it stands seven great hours in night, and spends half its course under the earth. And when it comes to the eastern approach in the eighth hour of the night it brings its lights and the crown of glory, and the sun burns (flames) outwardly more than fire.

Chapter 15

1 Then the elements of the sun, called Phoenixes and Chalkydri (Seraphim) break into song, therefore every bird flutters its wings, rejoicing at the giver of light, and they brake into song at the command of the Lord. (This is the Kadosh. Holy, Holy, Holy.)

2 The giver of light comes to illuminate the entire world, and the morning guard takes shape, which is the rays of the sun, and the sun of the earth goes out, and receives its luminance to light up the entire face of the earth, and they showed me this calculation of the sun's going.

3 And the great gates, which it enters into, are for the calculation of the hours of the year. For this reason the sun is a great creation, whose circuit lasts twenty-eight years, and begins again from the beginning.

(Note: For 29 February, which is the leap year day, to fall on a particular weekday, there is a 28-year (2 x 14 year) cycle. This forms a type of perpetual calendar. Also see 1 Enoch, Chap. 72-74.)

Chapter 16

1 Those men showed me the great course of the moon. There are twelve great gates that are crowned from west to east, by which the moon comes and goes in its customary times.

2 It goes in at the first gate to the western places of the sun, by the first gates with thirty-one days exactly, by the second gates with thirty-one days exactly, by the third with thirty days exactly, by the fourth with thirty days exactly, by the fifth with thirty-one days exactly, by the sixth with thirty-one days exactly, by the seventh with thirty days exactly, by the eighth with thirty-one days perfectly, by the ninth with thirty-one days exactly, by the tenth with thirty days perfectly, by the eleventh with thirty-one days exactly, by the twelfth with twenty-eight days exactly.

(Note: The sum of the days total 365 with the year beginning in March.)

3 And it goes through the western gates in the order and number of the eastern, and accomplishes the three hundred and sixty-five and a quarter days of the solar year, while the lunar year has three hundred fifty-four, and there twelve days lacking of the solar circle, which are the lunar epacts of the whole year.

(Note: epact | ē¸pakt | The number of days by which the solar year differs from the lunar year.

• the number of days into the moon's phase cycle at the beginning of the

solar (calendar) year.

Origin - mid 16th century. (Denoting the age of the moon in days at the beginning of the calendar year): from French épacte, via late Latin from Greek epaktai (hēmerai) 'intercalated (days).

4 The great circle also contains five hundred and thirty-two years.

(Note: The 532-year cycle is calculated from the creation of Adam, which, as we know, took place on Friday, March 1, 5508 B.C., which is the base date on which the entire calendar system of the Orthodox Church is founded. The cycles are laid out in the final sections of the Typikon, which is the book that dictates the services, and are the Paschalion Calendar sections. There are tables reflecting the 532 year cycle of the Church services, which consists of 19-year solar cycles multiplied by 28-day lunar cycles. There is a table that consists of 19 columns by 28 rows, giving the Paschal Key number or letter for each of the years of the 532-year cycle. Once you know the Paschal Key, you look up the details in the following section, which consists of 35 brief calendar synopses, one for each possible day that Pascha can fall. Each of these synopses actually consists of two services; one for regular years, and one for leap years.

5 The quarter (of a day) is omitted for three years, the fourth fulfills it exactly.

6 Because of this, they are taken outside of heaven for three years and are not added to the number of days, because they change the time of

the years to two new months toward completion, to two others toward the decrease.

7 And when the course through the western gates is finished, it returns and goes to the eastern to the lights, and goes this way day and night in its heavenly circles, below all circles, swifter than the heavenly winds, and spirits and elements and flying angels. Each angel has six wings.

8 In nineteen years it travels the course seven times.

Chapter 17

1 In the midst of the heavens I saw armed soldiers, serving the Lord, with drums and organs, with constant voice, with sweet voice, with sweet and unceasing voice and various singing, which it is impossible to describe, and which astonishes every mind, so wonderful and marvelous is the singing of those angels, and I was delighted listening to it.

Chapter 18

1 The men took me on to the fifth heaven and placed me, and there I saw many and countless soldiers, called Grigori, of human appearance, and their size (was) greater than that of great giants and their faces withered, and the silence of their mouths perpetual, and their was no service on the fifth heaven, and I said to the men who were with me: (See 2 Enoch 1:7)

(Note: The Greek transliteration egegoroi are the Watchers; a group of fallen angels who mated with mortal women and produced the Nephilim mentioned in the books of Jubilees, 1Enoch, and Genesis 6:4.)

2 Why are they so very withered and their faces melancholy, and their mouths silent, and why is there no service in this heaven?
3 And they said to me: These are the Grigori, who with their prince Satanail (Satan) rejected the Lord of Light. After them are those who are held in great darkness in the second heaven, and three of them went down on to earth from the Lord's throne, to the place Ermon, and broke through their vows on the shoulder of the hill Ermon and saw the daughters of men how good they are, and took to themselves wives, and fouled the earth with their deeds, who broke the law and mixing (with the women), giants are born and amazingly large men with great hatred.

(Note: The Hill of Ermon could be Mount Hermon, which is mentioned over a dozen times in the Bible.

4 And therefore God judged them with great judgment, and they weep for their brethren and they will be punished on the Lord's great day.
5 And I said to the Grigori: I saw your brethren and their works, and their great torments, and I prayed for them, but the Lord has condemned them to be under earth until this heaven and this earth shall end for ever.

6 And I said: Why do you stand there, brethren, and do not serve before the Lord's face, and have not put your services before the Lord's face? You could anger your Lord completely.

7 And they listened to my advice, and spoke to the four ranks in heaven. As I stood with those two men four trumpets sounded together with a loud voice, and the Grigori broke into song with one voice, and their voice went up before the Lord pitifully and touchingly.

Chapter 19

1 From there, those men took me and lifted me up on to the sixth heaven, and there I saw seven bands of angels, very bright and very glorious, and their faces shining more than the sun's shining, glistening, and there is no difference in their faces, or behavior, or manner of dress; and these make the orders, and learn the goings of the stars, and the alteration of the moon, or revolution of the sun, and the good administration of the world.

2 And when they see evildoing they make commandments and instruction, and make sweet and loud singing, and all (songs) of praise.

3 These are the archangels who are above angels, and they measure all life in heaven and on earth, and the angels who are (appointed) over seasons and years, the angels who are over rivers and sea, and who are over the fruits of the earth, and the angels who are over every grass, giving food to every and all living things, and the angels who write down all the souls of men, and all their deeds, and their

lives before the Lord's face. In their midst are six Phoenixes and six Cherubim and six six-winged ones continually singing with one voice, and it is not possible to describe their singing, and they rejoice before the Lord at his footstool.

Chapter 20

1 And those two men lifted me up from there on to the seventh heaven, and I saw there a very great light, and fiery troops of great archangels, incorporeal forces, and dominions, orders and governments, Cherubim and Seraphim, thrones and many-eyed ones, nine regiments, the Ioanit stations of light, and I became afraid, and began to tremble with great terror, and those men took me, and led me after them, and said to me:

2 Have courage, Enoch, do not fear, and showed me the Lord from afar, sitting on His very high throne. For what is there on the tenth heaven, since the Lord dwells there?

3 On the tenth heaven is God, in the Hebrew tongue he is called Aravat.

(Note: *The meaning of Ioanit is not clear. However, it may be derived from the transliteration of the name John. John means, "The Lord is Gracious." The meaning of Aravat is equally unclear but seems to mean, "Father of Creation."*

Each level of heaven represents or demonstrates a personality or part of the Godhead. One of the highest demonstrations of God's power and divinity is the power of Creation. It is found on the tenth level of heaven.)

4 And all the heavenly soldiers would come and stand on the ten steps according to their rank, and would bow down to the Lord, and would then return to their places in joy and bliss, singing songs in the unlimited light with soft and gentle voices, gloriously serving him.

(Note: Strong and fierce soldiers sing with soft, gentle voices, bowing and serving in bliss.)

Chapter 21

1 And the Cherubim and Seraphim standing around the throne, and the six-winged and many-eyed ones do not depart, standing before the Lord's face doing his will, and cover his whole throne, singing with gentle voice before the Lord's face: Holy, holy, holy, Lord Ruler of Sabaoth (Host / army), heavens and earth are full of Your glory.

2 When I saw all these things, the men said to me: Enoch, thus far we were commanded to journey with you, and those men went away from me and after that I did not see them.

3 And I remained alone at the end of the seventh heaven and became afraid, and fell on my face and said to myself: Woe is me. What has befallen me?

4 And the Lord sent one of his glorious ones, the archangel Gabriel, and he said to me: "Have courage, Enoch, do not fear, arise before the Lord's face into eternity, arise and come with me."

5 And I answered him, and said within myself: My Lord, my soul has departed from me due to terror and trembling, and I called to the men who led me up to this place. I relied on them, and it is with them that I can go before the Lord's face.

(Note: When speaking to God, Enoch "said within himself." He did not have to speak aloud.)

6 And Gabriel lifted me up like a leaf caught up by the wind, and he placed me before the Lord's face.

7 And I saw the eighth heaven, which is called in the Hebrew tongue Muzaloth (Zodiac), the changer of the seasons, of drought, and of wet, and of the twelve constellations of the circle of the firmament, which are above the seventh heaven.

8 And I saw the ninth heaven, which is called in Hebrew Kuchavim, where are the heavenly homes of the twelve constellations of the circle of the firmament.

Chapter 22

1 On the tenth heaven, which is called Aravoth, I saw the appearance of the Lord's face, like iron made to glow in fire, and it shone forth and casted out, emitting sparks, and it burned.

(Note: One possible meaning of Aravoth is "three times holy" or "holy, holy, holy."

2 In a moment of eternity I saw the Lord's face, but the Lord's face is indescribable, marvelous and very amazing, and very, very terrible.

3 And who am I to tell of the Lord's unspeakable being, and of his very wonderful face? I cannot tell the amount of his instructions, and the variety of voices. The Lord's throne is very great and not made with hands, and I cannot tell the number of those standing around him. There were troops of Cherubim and Seraphim, and they sang unceasingly. I cannot tell of his unchanging beauty. Who shall tell of the unpronounceable greatness of his glory?

4 And I fell prone and bowed down to the Lord, and the Lord with his lips said to me:

5 "Have courage, Enoch, do not fear, arise and stand before my face into eternity (stand before my face eternally / stand before my eternal face.)"

(Note: Enoch is out of and above time-space. Eternity is now and he can feel the timelessness of where he is. The language struggles to convey this fact.)

6 And the archangel Michael lifted me up, and led me to the Lord's face.

7 And the Lord said to his servants, testing them: Let Enoch stand before my face into eternity, and the glorious ones bowed down to the Lord, and said: Let Enoch go according to Your word.

8 And the Lord said to Michael: Go and take Enoch and remove his earthly garments, and anoint him with my sweet ointment, and put him into the garments of My glory.

9 And Michael did as the Lord told him. He anointed me, and dressed me, and the appearance of that ointment is more than the great light, and his ointment is like sweet dew, and its smell mild, shining like the sun's ray, and I looked at myself, and I was transformed into one of his glorious ones.

(Note: The number symbolism of ten is that of new starts at a higher level, new beginnings, and re-creation. This is apparent in the book of 3 Enoch, where Enoch's transfiguration into the angel Metatron is explained.)

10 And the Lord summoned one of his archangels, whose name is Pravuil, whose knowledge was quicker in wisdom than the other archangels, who wrote all the deeds of the Lord; and the Lord said to Pravuil: Bring out the books from my store-houses, and a reed of quick-writing, and give it to Enoch, and deliver to him the best and comforting books out of your hand.

(Note: Enoch is now an angel. He now has access to the heavenly records and the understanding to use the knowledge. A reed was used in writing much like a quill was used.)

Chapter 23

1 And he was explaining to me all the works of heaven, earth and sea, and all the elements, their passages and goings, and the sounding of the thunders, the sun and moon, the progression and changes of the stars, the seasons, years, days, and hours, as well as

the risings of the wind, the numbers of the angels, and the formation of their songs, and all human things, the tongue of every human song and life, the commandments, instructions, and sweet-voiced singings, and all things that are fitting to learn.

2 And Pravuil told me: All the things that I have told you, we have written. Sit and write all the souls of mankind, however many of them are born, and the places prepared for them to eternity. And he said, all souls are prepared for eternity, before the formation of the world.

3 And for both thirty days and thirty nights, and I wrote out all things exactly, and wrote three hundred and sixty-six books.

(Note: If all things were created in six days, then the souls of all people were created at that time. In Jewish mythology, the place that the souls were houses until birth was called the Guf (Guph). Each soul was created for a certain place, time, and destiny. According to one version of the myth, when the Guf (Guph) is emptied of souls, time ceases. In another version, when the last soul dies and returns to God, time will end. Enoch wrote 366 book in a 720 hour period containing information on all things, including, "all souls who are prepared for eternity, before the formation of the world.")

Chapter 24

1 And the Lord summoned me, and said to me: Enoch, sit down on my left with Gabriel.

2 And I bowed down to the Lord, and the Lord spoke to me: Enoch, beloved, all that you see, all things that are standing finished, I tell

you even before the very beginning, I created all things from non-being. I created the visible, physical things from the invisible, spiritual (world).

3 Hear, Enoch, and take in my words, for I have not told My angels My secret, and I have not told them their rise (beginnings), nor My endless realm, nor have they understood my creating, which I tell you today.

4 For before all things were visible (physical), I alone used to go about in the invisible, spiritual things, like the sun from east to west, and from west to east.

5 But even the sun has peace in itself, while I found no peace, because I was creating all things, and I conceived the thought of placing foundations, and of creating the visible, physical creation.

(Note: Overview of the heavens:

First heaven - , Enoch arrives on angel's wings. There are storehouses of snow and dew.

Second heaven - , Enoch finds a group of fallen angels. There is darkness and torture.

Third heaven - There are sweet flowers, trees, and fruit.

Fourth heaven – There are soldiers, heaven's army, and the progression of sun and moon.

Fifth heaven - The leaders of the fallen angels, the "Grigori" (Greek "Gregoroi," translating Mearim, the Hebrew word for watchers.) Three of them went down and had intercourse with the daughters of men, yielding giants, who became the source of enmity on earth.

Sixth heaven – Seven bands of angels and the ordering of the stars.

Seventh heaven, shows something unusual happening to Enoch when Gabriel puts Enoch in front of the throne of the Lord.

The Eighth, Ninth, and Tenth Heavens are thought to be later additions and not part of the original text.

Eighth heaven - "Muzaloth" -- Zodiac

Ninth heaven - "Kuchavim" -- heavenly bodies (stars).

Tenth heaven - "Aravoth" -- descriptions of God's face like that of iron made to glow in fire.

Enoch sees the "appearance of the Lord's face," but describes it as indescribable.

Pravuil, the archangel, is commanded to write down secret information about astronomy, climate, and language and give it over to Enoch. In other Enochian writings the same angel, also spelled "Penemue", is criticized for teaching humans to write.

Chapter 25

1 I commanded in the very lowest parts, that the visible, physical things should come down from the invisible, spiritual (realm), and Adoil came down very great, and I beheld him, and he had a belly of great light.

2 And I said to him: Become undone, Adoil, and let the visible, physical (universe) come out of you.

3 And he came undone, and a great light came out. And I was in the midst of the great light, and as there is born light from light, there

came forth a great age (eon / space of time), and showed all creation, which I had thought to create.

4 And I saw that it was good.

5 And I placed for myself a throne, and took my seat on it, and said to the light: Go up higher from here and station yourself high above the throne, and be a foundation to the highest things.

6 And above the light there is nothing else, and then I rose up and looked up from my throne.

(Note: Beginning with chapters 25 and 26, the book of 2 Enoch takes a rather Gnostic diversion. The Gnostics were a Christian sect that flourished around the 3rd century A.D. The Gnostic view of the Godhead borrowed heavily from the creation saga preached by Plato (circa 428 B.C. to 348 B.C.) The story of Adoil and the emanation of pure light from God, which brings about creation of the physical world, is similar to other Gnostic works. Gnosticism teaches that in the beginning a Supreme Being called The Father, The Divine All, The Origin, The Supreme God, or The Fullness, emanated the element of existence, both visible and invisible. His intent was not to create but, just as light emanates from a flame, so did creation shine forth from God. This manifested the primal element needed for creation.

This was the creation of Barbelo, who is the "Thought of God."
The Father's thought performed a deed and she was created from it. It is she who had appeared before him in the shining of his light. This is the first power which was before all of them and which was created from his mind. She is the Thought of the All and her light shines like his light. It is the

perfect power, which is the visage of the invisible. She is the pure, undefiled Spirit who is perfect. She is the first power. Adoil has that place is this myth.

It could be said that Barbelo was the creative emanation and, like the Divine All, is both male and female. It was the "agreement" of Barbelo and the Divine All, representing the union of male and female, that created the Christ Spirit and all the Aeons. In some renderings the word "Aeon" is used to designate an ethereal realm or kingdom. In other versions "Aeon" indicates the ruler of the realm. The Aeons of this world are merely reflections of the Aeons of the eternal realm. The reflection is always inferior to real.

In several Gnostic cosmologies the "living" world is under the control of entities called Aeons, of which Sophia is head. This means the Aeons influence or control the soul, life force, intelligence, thought, and mind. Control of the mechanical or inorganic world is given to the Archons.

The Archons were created by Sophia. Sophia, probably out of pride, tried to emulate the creative force of God by created an image of herself. Meaning that she wanted to produce an offspring, without either consort or the approval of her Father, God. As an aeon, she did have the power to do so, but she wasn't perfect like the Great Spirit, or like the other two perfect aeons, Barbelo and the Autogenes. Nevertheless, in her arrogance, she attempted to create and failed. She was horrified when she saw her creation, imperfect, bruthish creature with a lion-faced serpent with eyes of fire, whom she called Yaldabaoth.

Sophia cast her offspring out of pleroma (heaven), and hid her child within a thick cloud from the other aeons, because of her embarrassment and shame. Yaldabaoth was the first of the archon ("ruler") and he stole his mother's power, so that she wasn't able to escape from the cloud. Despite gaining Sophia's aeonic power, he was weak, but prideful, ambitious and power hungry.

Since the archons, including Yaldabaoth, were androgynous beings, Yaldabaoth fathered twelve archons, giving each a bit of his power. They were named Athoth, Harmas, Kalila-Oumbri, Yabel, Adonaiou (or Sabaoth), Cain, Abel, Abrisene, Yobel, Armoupieel, Melceir-Adonein and Belias. Seven archons would rule seven heavens and five in the abyss, which Yaldabaoth and the archons created. Each archon would rule a heaven (or the abyss), and created 365 angels to help them.

The archons rule the physical aspects of systems, regulation, limits, and order in the world. Both the ineptitude and cruelty of the Archons are reflected in the chaos and pain of the material realm.

(See the book, The Gnostic Scriptures, by Joseph Lumpkin, published by Fifth Estate.)

Although the above may be a digression from the text of 2 Enoch, it adds insight into the time frame and origins of its production. Gnostic influences were felt from the late first century to the early fourth century A.D. If the writer of this section of 2 Enoch was exposed to the Gnostic sect, it would conclusively make 2 Enoch a text with Christian influences.)

Chapter 26

1 And I summoned the very lowest a second time, and said: Let Archas come forth hard, and he came forth hard from the invisible, spiritual.

2 And Archas came forth, hard, heavy, and very red.

3 And I said: Be opened, Archas, and let there be born from you, and he came apart, and an age came forth, very great and very dark, bearing the creation of all lower things, and I saw that it was good and said to him:

4 Go down below, and make yourself solid, and be a foundation for the lower things, and it happened and he went down and stationed himself, and became the foundation for the lower things, and below the darkness there is nothing else.

(Note: Hard and heavy could be terms for "gravid" or pregnant, with birth being imminent. Archas could equate to "The Archons.")

Chapter 27

1 And I commanded that there should be taken from light and darkness, and I said: Be thick, and it became thick, and I spread it out with the light, and it became water, and I spread it out over the darkness, below the light, and then I made firm the waters, that is to say the bottomless (abyss), and I made foundation of light around the water, and created seven circles from inside, and made the water look like crystal, wet and dry, so it was like glass, and the circles

were around the waters and the other elements, and I showed each one of them its path, and the seven stars each one of them in its heaven, that they go the correct way, and I saw that it was good.

2 And I made separations between light and darkness in the midst of the water here and there, and I said to the light, that it should be the day, and to the darkness, that it should be the night, and there was evening and there was morning on the first day.

(Note: The foundation of light around the water that is like crystal is likely a reference to the sky. One belief at the time of writing was that the sky was an expanse of water like an endless sea.)

Chapter 28

1 And then I made firm the heavenly circle, and made that the lower water which is under heaven collect itself together into one whole (piece), and that the chaos become dry, and it became so.

2 Out of the waves I created hard and large rock, and from the rock I piled up the dry (land), and the dry (land) I called earth, and the middle of the earth I called the abyss, or the bottomless. I collected the sea in one place and bound it together with a yoke. *(Note: This is the bank or shoreline.)*

3 And I said to the sea: Behold I give you eternal limits, and you shall not break loose from your integral parts.

4 Thus I made the firmament hold together. This day I called the first-created, Sunday. (This, I call the first day of creation.)

Chapter 29

1 And for all the heavenly soldiers I made them the image and essence of fire, and my eye looked at the very hard, firm rock, and from the gleam of my eye the lightning received its wonderful nature, (which) is both fire in water and water in fire, and one does not put out the other, nor does the one dry up the other, therefore the lightning is brighter than the sun, softer than water and firmer than hard rock.

(Note: If the sky is made of water and lightning, which is fire, issues from the sky, then water and fire must exist together in a heavenly form.)

2 And from the rock I cut off a great fire, and from the fire I created the orders of the incorporeal (spiritual / non-physical) ten troops of angels, and their weapons are fiery and their raiment a burning flame, and I commanded that each one should stand in his order.
3 And one from out the order of angels, having violated the command he was given, conceived an impossible thought, to place his throne higher than the clouds above the earth so that he might become equal in rank to my power.
4 And I threw him out from the height with his angels, and he was flying in the air continuously above the bottomless (abyss).

(Note: We assume this ends the second day, although it is not mentioned.)

Chapter 30

1 On the third day I commanded the earth to make and grow great and fruitful trees, and hills, and seeds to sow, and I planted Paradise, and enclosed it, and placed armed guards in the form of my flaming angels, and in this way I created renewal.

2 Then came evening, and morning came of the fourth day.

3 On Wednesday, the fourth day, I commanded that there should be great lights on the heavenly circles.

4 On the first uppermost circle I placed the stars, Cronus, and on the second Aphrodite, on the third Ares, on the fifth Zeus, on the sixth Ermis (Hermes), on the seventh lesser the moon, and adorned it with the lesser stars.

(Note: The fourth heavenly circle is vacant. The Greek names for the heavenly bodies leave no doubt as to the influence of Greek words and ideas within this section of the text.)

5 And on the lower (parts) I placed the sun for the illumination of day, and the moon and stars for the illumination of night.

6 (And I set) the sun that it should go according to each of the twelve constellations , and I appointed the succession of the months and their names and lives, their thundering, and how they mark the hours, and how they should proceed.

7 Then evening came and morning came of the fifth day.

8 On Thursday, the fifth day, I commanded the sea, that it should bring forth fishes, and feathered birds of many varieties, and all animals creeping over the earth, going forth over the earth on four legs, and soaring in the air, of male and female sex, and every soul breathing the spirit of life.

(Note: Verse eight proclaims the creation of all souls breathing (inspired by) the spirit of life. The next verse proclaims the creation of man. This day filled the Guf (Guph) and incarnation begins in next.)

9 And there came evening, and there came morning of the sixth day.
10 On Friday, the sixth day, I commanded my wisdom to create man from seven consistent applications: one, his flesh from the earth; two, his blood from the dew; three, his eyes from the sun; four, his bones from stone; five, his intelligence from the swiftness of the angels and cloud; six, his veins and his hair from the grass of the earth; seven, his soul from my breath and from the wind.
11 And I gave him seven natures: to the flesh - hearing, the eyes for sight, to the soul - smell, the veins for touch, the blood for taste, the bones for endurance, to the intelligence - enjoyment.
12 I created a saying (speech) from knowing. I created man from spiritual and from physical nature, from both come his death and life and appearance. He knows speech like some created thing. He is small in greatness and great in smallness, and I placed him on earth, like a second angel, to be honorable, great and glorious. And I

appointed him as ruler to rule on earth and to have my wisdom, and there was none like him on earth of all my existing creatures.

13 And I appointed him a name made from the four components, from east, from west, from south, and from north. And I appointed for him four special stars, and I called his name Adam, and showed him the two ways, the light and the darkness, and I told him:

14 This is good, and that bad, so that I should learn whether he has love towards me, or hatred, and so that it would be clear who in his race loves me.

(Note: The Hebrew name of Adam means "man.)

15 For I have seen his nature, but he has not seen his own nature, and therefore by not seeing it he will sin worse, and I said, "After sin is there nothing but death?"

16 And I put sleep into him and he fell asleep. And I took from him a rib, and created him a wife, so that death should come to him by his wife, and I took his last word and called her name mother, that is to say, Eve.

Chapter 31

1 Adam has life on earth, and I created a garden in Eden in the east, so that he should observe the testament and keep the command.

2 I made the heavens open to him, so that he would see the angels singing the song of victory, and the light without shadow.

3 And he was continuously in paradise, and the devil understood that I wanted to create another world, because Adam was lord on earth, to rule and control it.

4 The devil is the evil spirit of the lower places, he made himself a fugitive from the heavens as the devil and his name was Satan. Thus he became different from the angels, but his nature did not change his intelligence as it applied to his understanding of righteous and sinful things.

5 And he understood his condemnation and the sin that he had committed before. Therefore he devised a thought against Adam, in which he entered and seduced Eve, but did not touch Adam.

6 But I cursed ignorance. However, what I had blessed before I did not curse. I did not curse man, nor the earth, nor other creatures. But I cursed man's evil results, and his works.

Chapter 32

1 I said to him: You are earth (dirt), and into the earth from where I took you, you shall go, and I will not destroy you, but send you back from where I took you.

2 Then I can again receive you at My second presence.

3 And I blessed all my creatures, both physical and spiritual. And Adam was five and half hours in paradise.

4 And I blessed the seventh day, which is the Sabbath, on which he rested from all his works.

(Note: The five and a half hours is tied to the 5500 years of punishment mentioned in the Books of Adam and Eve. See "The First and Second Books of Adam and Eve" by Joseph Lumpkin.)

Chapter 33

1 And I appointed the eighth day also, that the eighth day should be the first-created after my work, and that the first seven revolve in the form of the seventh thousand, and that at the beginning of the eighth thousand there should be a time of not-counting, endless, with neither years nor months nor weeks nor days nor hours.

(Note: A day is as a thousand years. This is a prophecy seems to indicate that after six thousand years there will be a thousand years of rest, then there will be timelessness.)

2 And now, Enoch, all that I have told you, all that you have understood, all that you have seen of heavenly things, all that you have seen on earth, all that I have written in books by my great wisdom, and all these things I have devised and created from the uppermost foundation to the lower and to the end, and there is no counselor nor inheritor to my creations.

3 I am eternal unto myself, not made with hands, and without change.

4 My thought is my own counselor, my wisdom and my word creates, and my eyes observe how all things stand here and tremble with terror.

5 If I turn away my face, then all things will be destroyed.

6 Apply your mind, Enoch, and know him who is speaking to you, and take the books there, which you yourself have written.

7 I give you Samuil and Raguil, who led you upward with the books, and go down to earth, and tell your sons all that I have told you, and all that you have seen, from the lower heaven up to my throne, and all the troops.

8 For I created all forces, and there is none that resists me and none that does not subject himself to me. For all subject themselves to my kingdom, and labor for my complete rule.

9 Give them the books of the handwriting, and they will read them and will know that I am the creator of all things, and will understand how there is no other God but me.

10 And let them distribute the books of your handwriting from children to children, generation to generation, nation to nation.

11 And Enoch, I will give you, my intercessor, the archangel Michael, for the writings of your fathers Adam, Seth, Enos, Cainan, Mahaleleel, and Jared your father.

Chapter 34

1 They have rejected my commandments and my yoke, therefore worthless seed has come up, not fearing God, and they would not bow down to me, but have begun to bow down to empty gods, and rejected my unity (oneness / sovereignty), and have piled the whole earth up with lies, offences, abominable lust with one another, and

all manner of other unclean wickedness, which are disgusting to even mention.

2 And therefore I will bring down a deluge upon the earth and will destroy all men, and the whole earth will crumble together into great darkness.

Chapter 35

1 You will see that from their seed shall arise another generation, long afterward, but of them many will be full of very strong desires that are never satisfied.

2 He who raises that generation shall reveal the books of your writing of your fathers to them. And He must point out the guardianship of the world to the faithful men and workers of my pleasure, who do not acknowledge my name in empty words.

3 And they shall tell another generation, and those others who, having read, shall afterward be glorified more than the first.

Chapter 36

1 Now, Enoch, I give you a period of thirty days to spend in your house, and tell your sons and all your household, so that all may hear from you what was spoken by my face, so that they may read and understand that there is no other God but me.

2 And that they may always keep my commandments, and begin to read and absorb the books of your writing.

3 And after thirty days I shall send my angel for you, and he will take you from earth and from your sons and bring you to me.

Chapter 37

1 And the Lord called upon one of the older angels who was terrible and menacing, and He placed him by me. He appeared white as snow, and his hands were like ice, having the appearance of great frost, and he froze my face, because I could not endure the terror of the Lord, just as it is not possible to endure a stove's fire or the sun's heat, or the frost of the air.

2 And the Lord said to me: Enoch, if your face is not frozen here, no man will be able to look at your face.

Chapter 38

1 And the Lord said to those men who first led me up: "Let Enoch go down on to earth with you, and await him until the determined day."

2 And by night they placed me on my bed.

3 But Methuselah was expecting my return and was keeping watch at my bed by day and night. And he was filled with awe when he heard my return, and I told him, "Let all my household come together, so that I may tell them everything."

Chapter 39

1 Oh my children, my loved ones, hear the advice of your father, as much as is according to the Lord's will.

2 I have been allowed to come to you today, and preach to you, not from my lips, but from the Lord's lips, all that is now, and was, and all that will be until judgment day.

3 For the Lord has allowed me to come to you so that you could hear the words of my lips, a man was made great for you. But I am one who has seen the Lord's face, and it was like iron made to glow from fire it sends forth sparks and burns.

4 You look upon my eyes now. They are the eyes of a man enlarged with meaning for you, but I have seen the Lord's eyes, shining like the sun's rays and filling the eyes of man with awe.

5 You see now, my children, the right hand of a man that helps you, but I have seen the Lord's right hand filling heaven as he helped me.

6 You see the scope of my work is like your own, but I have seen the Lord's limitless and perfect scope, which has no end.

7 You hear the words of my lips, as I heard the words of the Lord, and they are like constant and great thunder with hurling of clouds.

8 And now, my children, hear the lecture of the father of the earth. I will tell you how fearful and awful it is to come before the face of the ruler of the earth, and how much more terrible and awful it is to come before the face of the ruler of heaven, who is the judge of the quick and the dead, and of the controller of the heavenly troops. Who (of us) can endure that endless pain?

Chapter 40

1 And now, my children, I know all things, for this is from the Lord's lips, and my eyes have seen this, from beginning to end.

2 I know all things, and have written all things in the books, the heavens and their end, and their abundance, and all the armies and their marching.

3 I have measured and described the stars, the great innumerable multitude of them.

4 What man has seen their revolutions and their entrances? For not even the angels see their number, but I have written all their names.

5 And I measured the sun's circumference, and measured its rays, and counted the hours. I also wrote down all things that go over the earth. I have written down the things that are nourished, and all seed sown and unsown, which the earth produces, and all plants, and every grass and every flower, and their sweet smells, and their names, and the dwelling-places of the clouds, and their composition, and their wings, and how they carry rain and raindrops.

6 And I investigated all things, and described the road of the thunder and of the lightning, and they showed me the keys and their guardians, their rise, and the way they precede. They are let out gradually, in measure, by a chain. If they were not let out at a measured rate by a heavy chain their violence would hurl down the angry clouds and destroy all things on earth.

7 I described the treasure houses of the snow, and the storehouses of the cold and the frosty airs, and I observed the key-holders of the seasons. He fills the clouds with them, and it does not exhaust the treasure houses.

8 And I wrote down the resting places of the winds and observed and saw how their key-holders bear weighing-scales and measures.

First, they put them in one side of the weighing-scale, then in the other side they place the weights and let them out according to measure skillfully, over the whole earth, to keep the heavy winds from making the earth rock. (The wind blows and the earth hardens.) 9 And I measured out the whole earth, its mountains, and all hills, fields, trees, stones, rivers, all existing things I wrote down, the height from earth to the seventh heaven, and downwards to the very lowest hell, and the judgment-place, and the very great, open and weeping (gaping) hell.

10 And I saw how the prisoners are in pain, expecting the limitless judgment.

11 And I wrote down all those being judged by the judge, and all their judgment and sentences and all their works.

Chapter 41

1 And I saw throughout all time all the forefathers from Adam and Eve, and I sighed and broke into tears and spoke of the ruin and their dishonor.

2 And I sad, "Woe is me for my infirmity and for that of my forefathers," and thought in my heart and said:

3 "Blessed is the man who has not been born or who has been born and shall not sin before the Lord's face, because he will not come into this place, nor bear the yoke of this place on himself.

Chapter 42

1 I saw the key-holders and guards of the gates of hell standing like great serpents. And their faces were glowing like extinguishing lamps, and I saw their eyes of fire, and their sharp teeth. And I saw all of the Lord's works, how they are right, while some of the works of man are of limited good, and others bad, and in their works are those who are known to speak evil lies.

Chapter 43

1 My children, I measured and wrote out every work and every measure and every righteous judgment.

2 As one year is more honorable than another, so is one man more honorable than another. Some men are honored for great possessions, some for wisdom of heart, some for particular intellect, some for skillfulness, one for silence of lips, another for cleanliness, one for strength, another for beauty, one for youth, another for sharp wit, one for shape of body, another for sensibility, but let it be heard everywhere: There is none better than he who fears God. He shall be more glorious in time to come.

Chapter 44

1 The Lord created man with his hands in the likeness of his own face. The Lord made him small and great.

2 Whoever reviles the ruler's face hates the Lord's face, and has contempt for the Lord's face, and he who vents anger on any man without having been injured by him, the Lord's great anger will cut

him down, he who spits on the face of man reproachfully will be cut down at the Lord's great judgment.

3 Blessed is the man who does not direct his heart with malice against any man, and helps the injured and condemned, and raises up the broken down, and does charity to the needy, because on the day of the great judgment every weight, every measure and every makeweight will be as in the market, so they are hung on scales and stand in the market, and every one shall learn his own measure, and according to his measure shall take his reward.

(Note: Makeweight is something put on a scale to make up the required weight for a more precise measurement.)

Chapter 45

1 Whoever hurries to make offerings before the Lord's face, the Lord will hasten that offering by giving of His work.

2 But whoever increases his lamp before the Lord's face and makes a judgment that is not true, the Lord will not increase his treasure in the realm of the highest.

(Note: Whoever makes himself out to be more than he is and whoever judges others without truth or cause, the Lord will not reward in heaven.)

3 When the Lord demands bread, or candles, or the flesh of beasts, or any other sacrifice, it is nothing; but God demands pure hearts, and with all He does it is only the tests of man's heart.

Chapter 46

1 Hear, my people, and take in the words of my lips.

2 If any one brings any gifts to an earthly ruler, and has disloyal thoughts in his heart, and the ruler know this, will the ruler not be angry with him, and refuse his gifts, and give him over to judgment?

3 Or if one man makes himself appear good to another by deceit of the tongue, but has evil in his heart, then will the other person not understand the treachery of his heart, and condemned him, since his lie was plain to all?

4 And when the Lord shall send a great light, then there will be judgment for the just and the unjust, and no one shall escape notice.

Chapter 47

1 And now, my children, with your minds and your hearts, mark well the words of your father, which all have come to you from the Lord's lips.

2 Take these books of your father's writing and read them.

3 For there are many books, and in them you will learn all the Lord's works, all that has been from the beginning of creation, and will be until the end of time.

4 And if you will observe my writing, you will not sin against the Lord; because there is no other except the Lord in heaven, nor in earth, nor in the very lowest places, nor in the foundation.

5 The Lord has placed the foundations in the unknown, and has spread out heavens, both physical and spiritual; he anchored the

earth on the waters, and created countless creatures. Who has counted the water and the foundation of the mutable, (changeable, corruptible) or the dust of the earth, or the sand of the sea, or the drops of the rain, or the morning dew, or the wind's blowing (breathing)? Who has filled earth and sea, and the indestructible winter?

6 I (The Lord) cut the stars out of fire, and decorated heaven, and put it in their midst.

Chapter 48

1 The sun goes along the seven heavenly circles, which are the appointment of one hundred and eighty-two thrones. It goes down on a short day, and again one hundred and eighty-two. It goes down on a long day, and he has two thrones on which he rests, revolving here and there above the thrones of the months, from the seventeenth day of the month Tsivan it goes down to the month Thevan, from the seventeenth of Thevan it goes up.

(Note: The words Tsivan and Thevan refer to the summer and winter solstice, dividing the lengthening and shortening of days.
The sun goes in a sinusoidal wave, decreasing daylight time for 182 days and growing longer in daylight hours for 182 days, with an extra day, which is a long day. The total is 365 days.)

2 When it goes close to the earth, then the earth is glad and makes its fruits grow, and when it goes away, then the earth is sad, and trees and all fruits will not flower.

3 All this He measured, with good measurement of hours, and predetermined a measure by his wisdom, of the physical and the spiritual (realms).

4 From the spiritual realm he made all things that are physical, himself being spiritual.

5 So I teach you, my children, and tell you to distribute the books to your children, into all your generations, and among the nations who shall have the sense to fear God. Let them receive them, and may they come to love them more than any food or earthly sweets, and read them and apply themselves to them.

6 And those who do not understand the Lord, who do not fear God, who do not accept, but reject, who do not receive the books, a terrible judgment awaits these.

7 Blessed is the man who shall bear their yoke and shall drag them along, for he shall be released on the day of the great judgment.

Chapter 49

1 I swear to you, my children, but I do not swear by any oath, neither by heaven nor by earth, nor by any other creature created by God.

2 The Lord said: "There is no oath in Me, nor injustice, but only truth."

3 But there is no truth in men, so let them swear by the words, Yea, yea, or else, Nay, nay.

4 And I swear to you, yea, yea, that every man that has been in his mother's womb has had a place prepared for the repose of that soul, and a measure predetermined of how much it is intended that a man be tried (tested) in this world.

5 Yea, children, do not deceive yourselves, for there has been a place previously prepared for the soul of every man. *(This could be a statement of Predestination or foreknowledge.)*

Chapter 50

1 I have put every man's work in writing and none born on earth can remain hidden nor his works remain concealed.

2 I see all things.

3 Therefore, my children, spend the number of your days in patience and meekness so that you may inherit eternal life.

4 For the sake of the Lord, endure every wound, every injury, every evil word, and every attack.

5 If your good deeds are not rewarded but returned for ill to you, do not repay them to neither neighbor nor enemy, because the Lord will return them for you and be your avenger on the day of great judgment, so that there should be no vengeance here among men.

6 Whoever of you spends gold or silver for his brother's sake, he will receive ample treasure in the world to come.

7 Do not injure widows or orphans or strangers, for if you do God's wrath will come upon you.

Chapter 51

1 Stretch out your hands to the poor according to your strength.

2 Do not hide your silver in the earth.

3 Help the faithful man in affliction, and affliction will not find you in the time of your trouble.

4 And bear every grievous and cruel yoke that comes upon you, for the sake of the Lord, and thus you will find your reward in the Day of Judgment.

5 It is good to go morning, midday, and evening into the Lord's house, for the glory of your creator.

6 Because every breathing thing glorifies him, and every creature, both physical and spiritual, gives him praise. (Gives His praise back to Him.)

Chapter 52

1 Blessed is the man who opens his lips in praise of God of Sabaoth (Host / army) and praises the Lord with his heart.

2 Cursed is every man who opens his lips for the purpose of bringing contempt and slander to (of) his neighbor, because he brings God into contempt.

3 Blessed is he who opens his lips blessing and praising God.

4 Cursed before the Lord all the days of his life, is he who opens his lips to curse and abuse.

5 Blessed is he who blesses all the Lord's works.

6 Cursed is he who brings the Lord's creation into contempt.

7 Blessed is he who looks down and raises the fallen.

8 Cursed is he who looks to and is eager for the destruction of what is not his.

9 Blessed is he who keeps the foundations of his fathers that were made firm from the beginning.

10 Cursed is he who corrupts the doctrine of his forefathers.

11 Blessed is he who imparts peace and love.

12 Cursed is he who disturbs those that love their neighbors.

13 Blessed is he who speaks with humble tongue and heart to all.

14 Cursed is he who speaks peace with his tongue, while in his heart there is no peace but a sword.

15 For all these things will be laid bare in the scales of balance and in the books, on the day of the great judgment.

Chapter 53

1 And now, my children, do not say: "Our father is standing before God, and is praying for our sins. For there is there no helper for any man who has sinned.

2 You see how I wrote down all of the works of every man, before his creation, all that is done among all men for all time, and none can tell or relate my writing, because the Lord sees all imaginings of man, and how they are empty and prideful, where they lie in the treasure houses of the heart.

3 And now, my children, mark well all the words of your father that I tell you, or you will be regretful, saying: Why did our father not tell us?

(Note: although chapters 51 and 52 seem similar to the Sermon on the Mount, Chapter 53 offers no balance between mercy and justice. "There is no helper for any man who has sinned," is a statement excluding a savior. Scholars point to this verse to conclude 2 Enoch is a Jewish text. As stated before, 2 Enoch seems to be a Jewish text that was Christianized by additions and embellishment of the core text. Chapter 53 is part of the core Jewish text, likely written before the Christian sect. Verse 2 points to foreknowledge.)

Chapter 54

1 Let these books, which I have given you, be for an inheritance of your peace in that time that you do not understand things.

2 Hand them to all who want them, and instruct them, that they may see the Lord's very great and marvelous works.

Chapter 55

1 My children, behold, the day of my determined period (term and time) has approached.

2 For the angels who shall go with me are standing before me and urge me to my departure from you. They are standing here on earth, awaiting what has been told them.

3 For tomorrow I shall go up to heaven, to the uppermost Jerusalem, to my eternal inheritance.

4 Therefore I bid you to do the Lord's good pleasure before his face at all times.

(Note: The Jerusalem spoken of here is the spiritual Jerusalem, spoken of by John, coming down from heaven. The name, "Jerusalem" refers to the components of the actual name, which break down to mean "provision" and "peace".)

Chapter 56"

1 Methuselah answered his father Enoch, and said: What (food) is agreeable to your eyes, father, that I may prepare before your face, that you may bless our houses, and your sons, and that your people may be made glorious through you, and then that you may depart, as the Lord said?"

2 Enoch answered his son Methuselah and said: "Hear me, my child. From the time when the Lord anointed me with the ointment of his glory, there has been no food in me, and my soul remembers not earthly enjoyment, neither do I want anything earthly."

Chapter 57

1 My child Methuselah, summon all your brethren and all of your household and the elders of the people, that I may talk to them and depart, as is planned for me.

2 And Methuselah hurried, and summoned his brethren, Regim, Riman, Uchan, Chermion, Gaidad, and all the elders of the people before the face of his father Enoch; and he blessed them, and said to them:

Chapter 58

1 "Listen to me, my children, today.

2 In those days when the Lord came down to earth for Adam's sake, and visited all his creatures, which he created himself, after all these he created Adam, and the Lord called all the beasts of the earth, all the reptiles, and all the birds that soar in the air, and brought them all before the face of our father Adam.

3 And Adam gave names to all things living on earth.

4 And the Lord appointed him ruler over all, and subjected all things to him under his hands, and made them dumb and made them dull that they would be commanded by man, and be in subjection and obedience to him.

5 The Lord also created every man lord over all his possessions.

6 The Lord will not judge a single soul of beast for man's sake, but He judges the souls of men through their beasts in this world, for men have a special place.

7 And as every soul of man is according to number, similarly beasts will not perish, nor all souls of beasts which the Lord created, until the great judgment, and they will accuse man, if he did not feed them well.

Chapter 59

1 Whoever defiles the soul of beasts, defiles his own soul.

2 For man brings clean animals to make sacrifice for sin, that he may have cure for his soul.

3 And if they bring clean animals and birds for sacrifice, man has a cure. He cures his soul.

4 All is given you for food, bind it by the four feet, to make good the cure.

5 But whoever kills beast without wounds, kills his own souls and defiles his own flesh.

6 And he who does any beast any injury whatsoever, in secret, it is evil practice, and he defiles his own soul.

(Note: To kill without a wound is to inflict blunt force trauma - to beat them to death.)

Chapter 60

1 He who works the killing of a man's soul (he who murders), kills his own soul, and kills his own body, and there is no cure for him for all time.

2 He who puts a man in any snare (moral entrapment), shall stick himself in it, and there is no cure for him for all time.

3 He who puts a man in any vessel, his retribution will not be wanting at the great judgment for all time.

4 He who works dishonestly or speaks evil against any soul, will not make justice for himself for all time.

Chapter 61

1 And now, my children, keep your hearts from every injustice, which the Lord hates. Just as a man asks something for his own soul from God, so let him do the same to every living soul, because I know all things, how in the great time to come there is a great

inheritance prepared for men, good for the good, and bad for the bad, no matter the number.

2 Blessed are those who enter the good houses, for in the bad houses there is no peace or return from them.

3 Hear, my children, small and great! When man puts a good thought in his heart, it brings gifts from his labors before the Lord's face. But if his hands did not make them, then the Lord will turn away his face from the labor of his hand, and (that) man cannot find the labor of his hands.

4 And if his hands made it, but his heart murmurs (complains), and his heart does not stop murmurs incessantly, he does not have (gain) any advantage.

Chapter 62

1 Blessed is the man who, in his patience, brings his gifts with faith before the Lord's face, because he will find forgiveness of sins.

2 But if he takes back his words before the time, there is no repentance for him; and if the time passes and he does not of his own will perform what is promised, there is no repentance after death.

3 Because every work which man does before the time (outside the time he has promised it), is all deceit before men, and sin before God.

Chapter 63

1 When man clothes the naked and fills the hungry, he will find reward from God.

2 But if his heart complains, he commits a double evil; ruin of himself and of that which he gives; and for him there will be no finding of reward because of that.

3 And if his own heart is filled with his food and his own flesh is clothed with his own clothing, he commits contempt, and will forfeit all his endurance of poverty, and will not find reward of his good deeds. (If he is selfish and does not add to the economy of others...)

4 Every proud and pontificating man is hateful to the Lord, and every false speech is clothed in lies. It will be cut with the blade of the sword of death, and thrown into the fire, and shall burn for all time.

Chapter 64

1 When Enoch had spoken these words to his sons, all people far and near heard how the Lord was calling Enoch. They took counsel together:

2 Let us go and kiss Enoch, and two thousand men came together and came to the place called Achuzan, where Enoch was with his sons.

3 And the elders of the people with the entire assembly came and bowed down and began to kiss Enoch and said to him:

4 "Our father Enoch, may you be blessed by the Lord, the eternal ruler, and now bless your sons and all the people, that we may be glorified today before your face.

5 For you shall be glorified before the Lord's face for eternity, since the Lord chose you from among all men on earth, and designated you as the writer of all his creation, both physical and spiritual, and

you are redeemed from the sins of man, and are the helper of your household."

Chapter 65

1 And Enoch said to all his people: "Hear me, my children. Before all creatures were created, the Lord created the physical and spiritual things.

2 And then a long term passed. Then after all of that he created man in the likeness of his own form, and put eyes into him to see, and ears into him to hear, and a heart to reflect, and intellect to enable him to deliberate.

3 And the Lord saw all the works of man, and created all his creatures, and divided time. From time he determined the years, and from the years he appointed the months, and from the months he appointed the days, and of days he appointed seven.

4 And in those he appointed the hours, measured them out exactly, that man might reflect on time and count years, months, and hours, as they alternate from beginning to end, so that he might count his own life from the beginning until death, and reflect on his sin and write his works, both bad and good. No work is hidden from the Lord, so that every man might know his works and never transgress all his commandments, and keep my writing from generation to generation.

5 When all creation, both physical and spiritual, as the Lord created it, shall end, then every man goes to the great judgment, and then all time shall be destroyed along with the years. And from then on there

will be neither months nor days nor hours. They will run together and will not be counted.

6 There will be one eon (age), and all the righteous who shall escape the Lord's great judgment, shall be collected in the great eon. For the righteous the great eon (age) will begin, and they will live eternally, and there will be no labor, nor sickness, nor humiliation, nor anxiety, nor need, nor brutality, nor night, nor darkness, but great light among them.

7 And they shall have a great indestructible wall, and a paradise that is bright and eternal, for all mortal things shall pass away, and there will be eternal life.

(Note: an eon is one billion years but is used to mean a very long but indefinite period of time. The word "eternal" means "unchanging, incorruptible, immortal." The word used for "mortal" is the opposite of "eternal", thus, "mortal, corruptible, changing.")

Chapter 66

1 And now, my children, keep your souls from all injustice the Lord hates.

2 Walk before his face with great fear (respect) and trembling and serve him only.

3 Bow down to the true God, not to dumb idols, but bow down to his likeness, and bring all just offerings before the Lord's face. The Lord hates what is unjust.

(Note: This is an odd command issued by Enoch, that the people are not to bow to dumb idols but are to bow to the likeness or similitude of God. This section was likely added by Christians after the fourth century A.D.)

4 For the Lord sees all things; when man takes thought in his heart, then he counsels the intellects, and every thought is always before the Lord, who made firm the earth and put all creatures on it.

5 If you look to heaven, the Lord is there; if you take thought of the sea's deep and all under the earth, the Lord is there.

6 For the Lord created all things. Bow not down to things made by man, leaving the Lord of all creation, because no work can remain hidden before the Lord's face.

7 Walk, my children, in long-suffering, in meekness, honesty, in thoughtfulness, in grief, in faith and in truth. Walk in (rely on) promises, in (times of) illness, in abuse, in wounds, in temptation, in nakedness, in privation, loving one another, until you go out from this age of ills, that you become inheritors of endless time.

8 Blessed are the just who shall escape the great judgment, for they shall shine forth more than the sun sevenfold, for in this world the seventh part is taken off from all, light, darkness, food, enjoyment, sorrow, paradise, torture, fire, frost, and other things; he put all down in writing, that you might read and understand.

Chapter 67

1 When Enoch had talked to the people, the Lord sent out darkness on to the earth, and there was darkness, and it covered those men

standing with Enoch, and they took Enoch up on to the highest heaven, where the Lord is. And there God received him and placed him before His face, and the darkness went off from the earth, and light came again.

2 And the people saw and did not understand how Enoch had been taken, and they glorified God, and found a scroll in which was written "The God of the Spiritual." Then all went to their dwelling places.

Chapter 68

1 Enoch was born on the sixth day of the month Tsivan (the first month of the year), and lived three hundred and sixty-five years.

2 He was taken up to heaven on the first day of the month Tsivan and remained in heaven sixty days.

3 He wrote all these signs of all creation, which the Lord created, and wrote three hundred and sixty-six books, and handed them over to his sons and remained on earth thirty days, and was again taken up to heaven on the sixth day of the month Tsivan, on the very day and hour when he was born.

4 As every man's nature in this life is dark, so are also his conception, birth, and departure from this life.

5 At what hour he was conceived, at that hour he was born, and at that hour also he died.

6 Methuselah and his brethren, all the sons of Enoch, made haste, and erected an altar at that place called Achuzan, where Enoch had been taken up to heaven.

7 And they took sacrificial oxen and summoned all people and sacrificed the sacrifice before the Lord's face.

8 All people, the elders of the people and the whole assembly came to the feast and brought gifts to the sons of Enoch.

9 And they made a great feast, rejoicing and making merry three days, praising God, who had given them such a sign through Enoch, who had found favor with him, and that they should hand it on to their sons from generation to generation, from age to age.   Amen.

(Note: Enoch was born on the 6th day of Tsivan. Tsivan is the first month of the year. The sum is seven, one of the holy numbers. He lived 365 years. One year of years. He remained in heaven 60 days. Six is the number of man, which always falls short of God.)

The Short Version Ends Here

The wife of Nir was Sopanim. She was sterile and never had at any time given birth to a child by Nir.

Sopanim was in her old age and in the last days (time) of her death. She conceived in her womb, but Nir the priest had not slept with her from the day that that the Lord had appointed him to conduct the liturgy in front of the face of the people.

When Sopanim saw her pregnancy, she was ashamed and embarrassed, and she hid herself during all the days until she gave

85

birth. Not one of the people knew about it. When 282 days had been completed, and the day of birth had begun to approach, Nir thought about his wife, and he called her to come to him in his house, so that he might converse with her. *(282 days is about 9.4 30-day-months.)*

Sopanim came to Nir, her husband; and, behold, she was pregnant, and the day appointed for giving birth was drawing near. Nir saw her and became very ashamed. He said to her, "What is this that you have done, O wife? Why have you disgraced me in front of the face of these people? Now, depart from me and go back to where you began this disgrace of your womb, so that I might not defile my hands in front of The Face of The Lord on account of you and sin."

Sopanim spoke to her husband, Nir, saying, "O my lord! Look at me. It is the time of my old age, the day of my death has arrived. I do not understand how my menopause and the barrenness of my womb have been reversed." But Nir did not believe his wife, and for the second time he said to her, "Depart from me, or else I might assault you, and commit a sin in front of the face of The Lord."

And after Nir had spoken to his wife, Sopanim, she fell down at Nir's feet and died. Nir was extremely distressed and said to himself, "Could this have happened because of my words? And now, merciful is The Eternal Lord, because my hand was not upon her."

The archangel Gabriel appeared to Nir, and said to him, "Do not think that your wife Sopanim has died due to your error? This child, which is to be born from her, is a righteous fruit, and one whom I shall receive into paradise so that you will not be the father of a gift of God."

Nir hurried and shut the door of his house. He went to Noah, his brother, and he reported to him everything that had happened in connection with his wife. Noah hurried to the room of his brother. The appearance of his brother's wife was as if she were dead but her womb was at the same time giving birth.

Noah said to Nir, "Don't let yourself be sorrowful, Nir, my brother! Today the Lord has covered up our scandal, because nobody from the people knows this. Now let us go quickly and bury her, and the Lord will cover up the scandal of our shame." They placed Sopanim on the bed, wrapped her around with black garments, and shut the door. They dug a grave in secret.

When they had gone out toward the grave, a child came out from Sopanim's dead body and sat on the bed at her side. Noah and Nir came in to bury Sopanim and they saw the child sitting beside Sopanim's dead body and he was wiping his clothing. Noah and Nir were very terrified with a great fear, because the child was physically fully developed. The child spoke with his lips and blessed The Lord. Noah and Nir looked at him closely, saying, "This is from the Lord, my brother." The badge of priesthood is on his chest, and it is glorious in appearance. Noah said to Nir, "God is renewing the priesthood from blood related to us, just as He pleases."

Noah and Nir hurried and washed the child, they dressed him in the garments of the priesthood, and they gave him bread to eat and he ate it. And they called him Melchizedek.

Noah and Nir lifted up the body of Sopanim, and took the black garment off of her and washed her. They clothed her in exceptionally bright garments and built a grave for her. Noah, Nir, and Melchizedek came and they buried her publicly. Then Noah said to his brother Nir, "Take care of this child in secret until the proper time comes, because all of the people on earth will become treacherous and they will begin to turn away from God. Having become completely ignorant (of God), when they see him, they will put him to death in some way."

Then Noah went away to his own place, and there came great lawlessness that began to become abundant over all the earth in the days of Nir. And Nir began to worry greatly about the child saying, "What will I do with him?" And stretching out his hands toward heaven, Nir called out to The Lord, saying, " It is miserable for me, Eternal Lord, that all of this lawlessness has begun to become abundant over all the earth in my lifetime! I realize how much nearer our end is because of the lawlessness of the people. And now, Lord, what is the vision about this child, and what is his destiny, or what will I do for him, so that he will not be joined along with us in this destruction?"

The Lord took notice of Nir and appeared to him in a night vision. And He said to him, "Nir, the great lawlessness which has come about on the earth I shall not tolerate anymore. I plan to send down a great destruction onto the earth. But do not worry about the child, Nir. In a short while I will send My archangel Gabriel and he will take the child and put him in the paradise of Edem. He will not perish along with those who must perish. As I have revealed it, Melchizedek will be My priest to all holy priests, I will sanctify him and I will establish him so that he will be the head of the priests of the future."

(Note: Edem means, "God will save." It is assumed Edem is Eden.)

Then Nir arose from his sleep and blessed The Lord, who had appeared to him saying: "Blessed be The Lord, The God of my fathers, who has approved of my priesthood and the priesthood of my fathers, because by His Word, He has created a great priest in the womb of Sopanim, my wife. For I have no descendants. So let this child take the place of my descendants and become as my own son. You will count him in the number of your servants."

"Therefore honor him together with your servants and great priests and me your servant, Nir. And behold, Melchizedek will be the head of priests in another generation. I know that great confusion has come and in confusion this generation will come to an end, and everyone will perish, except that Noah, my brother, will be preserved for procreation. From his tribe, there will arise numerous people, and Melchizedek will become the head of priests reigning over a royal people who will serve you, O Lord."

It happened when the child had completed 40 days in Nir's tent, The Lord said to the archangel Gabriel, "Go down to the earth to Nir the priest, and take the child Melchizedek, who is with him. Place him in the paradise of Edem for preservation. For the time is already approaching, and I will pour out all the water onto the earth, and everything that is on the earth will perish. And I will raise it up again, and Melchizedek will be the head of the priests in that generation." And Gabriel hurried, and came flying down when it was night when Nir was sleeping on his bed that night.

Gabriel appeared to him and said to him, "The Lord says: "Nir! Restore the child to me whom I entrusted to you." But Nir did not realize who was speaking to him and he was confused. And he said, "When the people find out about the child, they will seize him and kill him, because the heart of these people are deceitful before The Lord." And he answered Gabriel and said, "The child is not with me, and I don't know who is speaking to me."

Gabriel answered him, " Nir, do not be afraid. I am the archangel

Gabriel. The Lord sent me to take your child today. I will go with him and I will place him in the paradise of Edem." Then Nir remembered the first dream and believed it. He answered Gabriel, "Blessed be The Lord, who has sent you to me today! Now bless your servant Nir! Take the child and do to him all that has been said to you." And Gabriel took the child, Melchizedek on his wings in that same night, and he placed him in the paradise of Edem. Nir got up in the morning, and he went into his tent and did not find the child. There was great joy and grief for Nir because he felt the child had the place of a son.

The Lord said to Noah, "Make an ark that is 300 cubits in length, 50 cubits in width and in 30 cubits height. Put the entrance to the ark in its side; and make it with two stories in the middle" The Lord God opened the doors of heaven. Rain came onto the earth and all flesh died.

Noah fathered 3 sons: Shem, Ham and Japheth. He went into the ark in his six hundredth year. After the flood, he lived 350 years. He lived in all 950 years, according to The Lord our God.
To our God be Glory always, now and eternally. AMEN.

About the Author

Joseph Lumpkin obtained his Doctorate of Ministry from Battlefield Baptist Institute. He has written for various newspapers and has authored numerous books, including the best selling book, The Lost Book of Enoch, a Comprehensive Transliteration." He now appears on radio and television shows and writes in the rural tranquility of Alabama.

Look for other books by Joseph Lumpkin, including:

Banned From The Bible: Books Banned, Rejected, And Forbidden
ISBN-10: 193358047X

The Lost Books of the Bible: The Great Rejected Texts
ISBN-10: 1933580666

Joseph B. Lumpkin

Fallen Angels, the Watchers, and the Origins of Evil
ISBN: 1933580100

The Gospel of Thomas: A Contemporary Translation
ISBN: 0976823349

The Book of Jubilees; The Little Genesis, The Apocalypse of Moses
ISBN: 1933580097

www.ingramcontent.com/pod-product-compliance
Lightning Source LLC
Chambersburg PA
CBHW071103090426
42737CB00013B/2459